THE PSYCHOLOGY OF GROWTH

ACKNOWLEDGEMENT

Before I begin, let me introduce myself. I am just a man who has grown up with a variety of experiences. I am just going to summarize them in a prolonged story. Just like everybody else, I breathe oxygen and just like everybody else I have my everyday struggles. As I began to pen down my thoughts, I began to think whether anybody will be willing to read what I had to say. Then I realized, penning down one's own thoughts is a way to escape some reality. And the question then arises, why we want to escape reality at all.

This book is dedicated to all the people who have come out strong or are looking for somewhere to start. I don't like to give examples of successful people and reiterate what they have done and what should we be doing to reach great success. I always wanted to highlight things which are natural and occurring in our everyday lives. This book tries to highlight the little things in life through certain experiences I have had, or I have had the joy of living those experiences through the people around me.

To thank a special few, I would like to dedicate this book to my **parents** and my close friends **Aditi, Damayanti, Dhiman, Mainak, Monisha, Sarbojit, Snehasish, Syamantak** and **Tuhin**. I would also like to thank all my **teachers** and all my **friends** who have helped me in growing up. Thanks to all of you for your support in different phases of my life throughout the years and all of you have taught me valuable lessons which brings me to this book.

THE BIRTH

All of a sudden we appear in this world and woof we go. We start our lives with a wail and there begins our journey. The initial stages of our lives are the ones that are generally blissful if we are lucky. Care is showered on us irrespective of whether we are born rich or poor. I have been fortunate enough to be born in an economically stable family and as a result narrating the other side of the story will be fairly difficult for me.

To begin my story, the moment I was born, there were few drops of rain that fell and disappeared. Some people thought it to be a good sign. (How good that sign was will never be found out till my death as that is where a part of my journey will end. Yes a part of my journey). And there it was a journey that began.

The objective of my writing is not to highlight my life. I am sorry to disappoint you here if you thought otherwise. So okay, I won't waste another second and get straight back to the point.

In life, the moment we begin our life, we are thrust into this world to survive. The wailing indicates that we have just announced our presence in this world. Why we cry will have several thousand explanations but from my perspective it is the birth of the 5 children within us. So what do I talk about here? I feel the moment we are born, we develop our sensory organs (which are also 5 in number) but we are also born with 5 different personalities. This is again completely my opinion so you may agree to disagree. Let's list them out one by one and let us delve deep into what they could possibly transform into.

1. **Honesty:** The first personality that I personally feel we are inherently born with is the trait of honesty. When we are a child just after birth we try to make our presence felt by crying. There are no inhibitions to it. We are not exposed to the world and hence we don't fear it. Whatever we do, we just do. A total honest actions are always taken. For example, we want to pee in the bed, we do it. We don't take into consideration anything. You might wonder how it is linked with honesty. In my humble opinion, honesty refers to one doing what is right without thinking about the consequences of it. Now what is this term of doing right? This again is debatable. What is right for me may not be right for you. Honestly speaking, infants always feel they are right. More on this, later. (You will keep reading this line several times.)

2. **Intelligence:** The second personality that a child is born with is intelligence. Intelligence when loosely defined will determine how the child perceives the world. A child has the extreme capability to visualize things. And each child has the ability to view things differently. It is similar to the analogy of two people standing at two ends of the number 6 or 9. One of the people might view it as 6 whereas the other might blissfully view it as 9. We need to remember none of them are correct here. And the question is not at all about being correct. It is more about knowing how the intelligence of a person shapes his/her personality.

3. **Anger:** Now you may wonder how this is even a personality. Anger is itself a personality and with time our anger gets converted into many different emotions which I will keep highlighting throughout. You might wonder, how is a child angry and how is it even related to the personality of the child when the child is just born? Well, some kids are furious that they entered this world, they cry more. They are not willing to adjust to this world the moment they are born. On the other hand, some kids will sob when they are born. A clear illustration of a different personality traits developing in them. So the thing that remains to be seen is how this angry child gets converted into a proper human being. Again the word proper is debatable as it differs from person to person but at this point of time, let us assume the child has an angry personality too.

4. **Adjustment:** This personality trait is inculcated within the child from the moment the child is born. A child tries to adapt to its surroundings. It tries to figure out the reason for its existence from the very beginning. The moment a child tries to think for itself, it tries to think keeping in mind the environment. So in a way he is trying to adjust. This is synonymous with how a child keeps crying till it actually gets into a comfort zone. The child keeps on crying trying to adjust to its environment. If that environment is not provided to the child, he will not continue to cry forever but will stop after sometime. The body seeks adjustment and tries to put a control chain that will prevent the child from wailing away all the time. This develops the adjustment personality in the child.

5. **Ignorance:** This personality of the child is the fiercest of them all. A child can decide to entirely ignore its environment. By deciding, I don't mean a concise logical decision making process exists in the child, but rather the skills to ignore certain experiences. We choose to react to certain situations in life in a particular way. The reason for

the same will vary but a lot of it depends on how we are brought up from our childhood. But this personality within us has a strong influence of what we become and how we react to certain situations. As I mentioned before, when a child wails, he/she has very little idea of the consequences it will have on the environment. This blissfully points out the ignorance in the child's personality development.

As soon as we are born, we start fighting and combating. Well this may sound like a very negative way to start a story but let's be blatant to the facts here. We start adjusting and coping up with the environment. This kind of develops the overall personality of the child. How a child responds becomes the way how the child will react to different situations in life. With the beginning of life form, there becomes a need to explore. How this need begins to manifest away can be seen in the later part of the life. The personalities I have mentioned gets distributed in a person once they become adults. The dominance of one personality over the other determines the person's overall attitude towards life.

The birth of a child is itself an evolutionary process. And an evolutionary process begins with adaption to change. Responding to change is itself an arduous task one must undergo even though the change maybe for the better. For example, you are told that you will be given your own chauffeur driven car for your travel to office. You, in the past, were travelling by public transport often reaching late. Now on the immediate go this sudden change will look blissful to most people but the person on the other hand might resist change thinking that he will have to do more work because he will now reach on time. Something which looks seemingly best to someone may not turn out to be the best alternative for that person to have. Have you ever experienced that something that you badly wanted lost its value once you got it? This is where life reaches the trigger point for evolution.

As I mentioned before that life begins with combat. This combat gets evolved over time and that is passed onto our future generations where they inherently develop the ability to adjust to the environment that they are born in. There is an inherent problem with evolution. Some changes are good and some are bad. To be honest, birth is not the beginning of a process. It is just a part of an iterative process that has been existing over millions of years. As soon as we are born, there are expectations and reactions that are formed around our birth. People surrounding a birth can be happy, can be sad and it can cause multiple ripples across different lives. Let me elaborate. Maybe the parents were expecting a girl child and a boy was born. That will give out a different reaction. Maybe you were born as a twin. Maybe the birth process itself was not called for. (I hope you get the drift, else it doesn't matter). The point of elucidating such stuff is that life itself is unpredictable to begin with. The transition from birth to a toddler to a kid is an interesting process. A child develops certain personalities with respect to the mix of personalities he/she is born with which I have already mentioned.

I won't delve into much of the evolutionary process that takes place just after the birth of the child. I will be rather talking about how the personality of a child gets developed with time. Moving on to the next chapter.

EARLY YEARS

As the child starts growing, he has a very inquisitive nature inbuilt. The child questions everything he sees, questions all the responses he gets and is often deeply involved in questioning the very self of existence. These early years of childhood will see some prominent characteristics in the child. Let's break them down into a few of the key observable characteristics.

1. **Determination:** Any child will have a lot of determination about what they want. You give them something that they don't want, they will start wailing. This attribute kind of goes to the adjust personality that I had been talking about. But in this case it is just the lack of adjustment. Now you may wonder that I am conflicting myself, but I believe, when we are born our adjustment quotient (let's innovate this term here) are susceptible to a lot of changes. Let's illustrate this by a graph. I will introduce a lot of quotient throughout this book and for simplicity let's assume that the maximum reachable quotient is 100. Now to make things more visual, let's describe how this quotient of adjustment varies in a child.

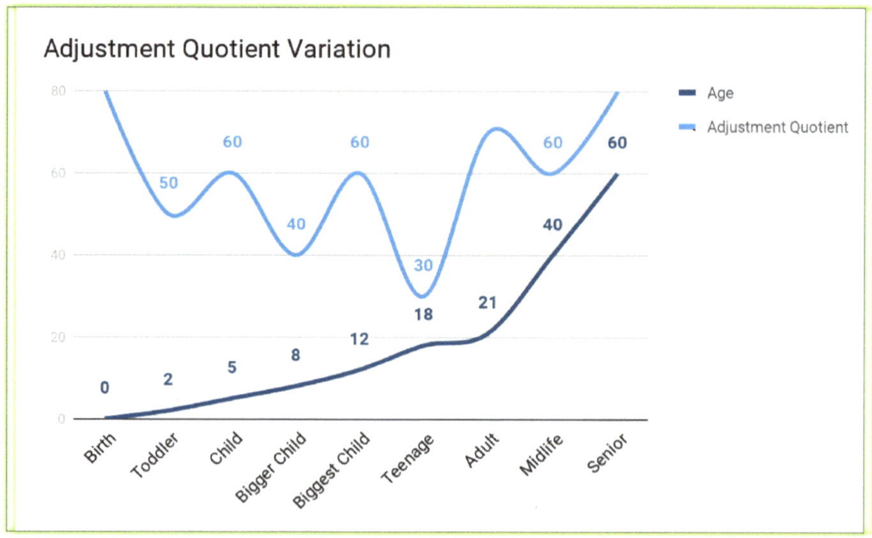

This graph is what I feel kind of depicts how the adjustment quotient develops in most of us. This is a generic graph. Don't ask for a scientific basis behind this. It is rather my observation and I am here to cite the aspects which kind of makes me believe how this graph is formed.

As I have mentioned before, we are trying to adjust from the moment we are born. I believe the moment we are born we are trying to adjust to the environment into which we are suddenly thrown in. In other words, we are trying to get a feel for the world. As we become a toddler, we kind of get a bit adjusted to the world and know things a little bit better although very little. This lets us think that we can have our way. And this makes the toddler kind of less adjust to the environment. He starts seeking attention to all the little things he wants. And when he doesn't get it, he feels the world is unfair and then keeps begging and fighting for it. This can be easily cited as the development of the entitlement within the child. He starts feeling entitled. And he also starts feeling narcissistic. (Too early, but still).

Now comes a key development to the child psychology. If the child is continuously provided with what he wants at this tender age, the child becomes more narcissistic and entitled and it will have a severe impact in the later stages of his life. So it is important to take care of the child at this phase of his life. It is very important to say no to some of his demands so that he can develop the ability to adjust and get that adjustment quotient to improve.

Once the toddler becomes a child, he has already faced several rejections to some of his demands. By this time the child has developed the psychology that it is not possible to get whatever he wants and as a result his adjustment quotient kind of improves. It is worthy to note that it still doesn't reach the level that the child had when he was born. This is mainly because when he was born, the subconscious psychology was that he was no one in this world. But now at roughly around 6 years of age, the child has already developed an identity. He has his own name to which he responds to once he is called by someone, he has his own set of toys, and he has his own set of things to deal with, although they are not many or a very expensive affair. The identity of one's self is both harmful and necessity. More on this, later. (Yes I had to use it again).

As the child goes to the bigger child phase (Yes, kind of inventing the term here), the child is suddenly hit with the fact that he has an identity crisis. The interaction he has with people kind of increases and he starts feeling the need to be within the group. If the child has been nurtured with the right values, he will find it easy to mingle with others. The innate human nature is to combine and cooperate with people. This is how in the ancient times, humans used to go together for hunting food. The very need for existing in a group kind of increases and to stand out in the group increases further. In the primary school stage of the child, the child now gets adjusted with the facts of human existence. He wants to stand out in the crowd. The early need arises. He wants to be the best at something that he is doing and he wants to get it done by any means. This has an implication on another quotient other than the adjustment quotient. This is the honesty quotient. Let's see how the honesty quotient pans out in a person's life.

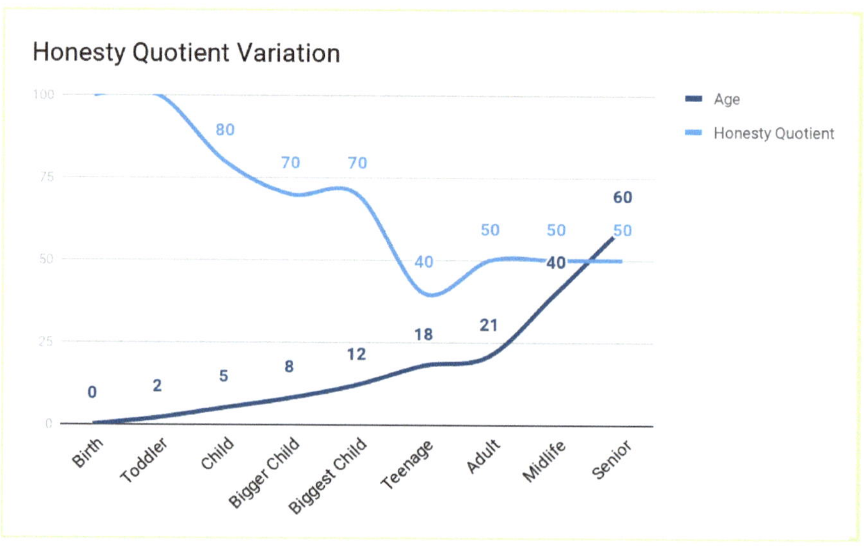

The honesty quotient is kind of different in a person's entire life. These values are obviously very subjective but it is important to note the pattern that is kind of existing in human beings as they grow older.

As humans are born, they don't have the need to lie. The need to lie is often a reactionary force. The need to be dishonest arises from the fact that something is at stake. More on this, later.

As we can see from the graph, it is clear that the honesty quotient kind of decreases in people's lives and kind of saturates at the later stages of life. This is because the full personality of the person is kind of developed. Don't be fooled by the value of 50 as an honesty quotient which might indicate that the people lie 50% of the time. As I said the value is arbitrary and it merely kind of depicts the finalization of the characteristics and personality of the human beings. If a person often tells a lie during 30 years of age, chances are he will maintain that often telling of a lie even at 60 years of age. This is how the person becomes wired to the environment. It is essential for the person to build up good values in the very beginning phase of his life so that the person's honesty quotient saturates at a very high level. It is impossible to be 100% honest. We all have the inherent quality to lack a little bit of honesty. And that to me, is perfectly fine. As long as you are not hurting anyone or your dishonesty has bad repercussions on yourself as well as the people around you, do whatever the hell you want.

2. Carelessness: Kind of paradoxical here. I mentioned about determination. On the contrary, carelessness is also a habit that develops in the early years. And this again kind of varies from person to person. This nature of carelessness is surprisingly a necessary evil. This nature of the child helps him get rid of the entitlement that he had developed in the little time he has been existing in the world. You might wonder how? Well the fact remains is that the carelessness in the child will result into a lot of mistakes he will do. And by the rule of nature, he will be reprimanded for doing all those mistakes. This kind of develops the neural thinking model the child will have. It is apparently very simple. Probably it can be explained by a flowchart.

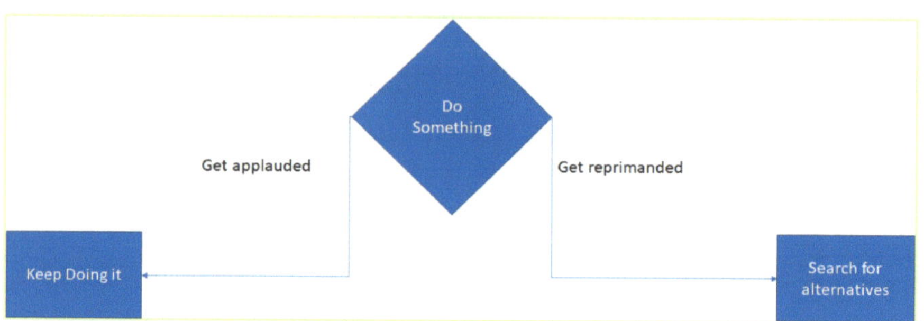

But it isn't as simple as the above flowchart. The problem is not with the "Get Applauded" side of things but rather with the "Get Reprimanded" side of things. Once the child gets reprimanded, he immediately doesn't start to believe what he did is wrong. He will keep doing it until he feels his ego arising out of his carelessness is actually satisfied. This is where the importance of nurturing of proper value comes in. It may seem that a child doesn't have an ego, but the answer to that is no. You might wonder why ego is not included in my classification of different personalities. Ego is kind of a culmination of many factors. Inherently the factor of ego is not there in a human being. The factor of ego gets build along with time. So the fact of the matter remains that it is not an intrinsic quantity which should be measured.

3. Innovativeness: Now this is something which is funny. You will find a lot of acts which are totally illogical to a grown up done by the child. This is because the child's mind has not been filled up with the world's norm of things. It is important to carefully allow the child to express. If the child at this fragile stage of life is not allowed to express freely, the child will develop the mentality of hiding things. This in turn will result into hitting of the honesty quotient that the child will develop and as a result the saturation value for the honesty quotient will settle down at a lower value. If the adult monitoring the child, finds that the child is doing something utterly ridiculous, only then the adult should intervene and try and simplify the things for the child without actually scolding the child. Reprimanding the child and being harsh to a child is not at all necessary. As I mentioned before, a child is born with the intelligence personality which tries to analyze things. Some things will not make sense for the child at that tender age and yet he might end up doing it. It is important to reason out with the child rather than commanding the child about what is right and what is wrong. It is important for the child to express freely without any inhibitions and without creating a troubled mindset for the child. As we grow older, the child in us kind of withers away. This implies the innovative ideas that we are going to have will kind of become less and less innovative and become more of a trained social aspect. More on this, later.

The inner artist in a child also develops with this innovativeness aspect. The child scans the environment and tries to articulate things in his own natural way exercising his own little judgments in whatever he does. I remember in my case, I had painted a mountain totally blue. The colour of the sky and the colour of the mountain were same. My mother was flabbergasted at the situation and kind of asked me the reason behind the same. I had replied casually that, I had seen the mountains being blue in a TV Cartoon show called "Heidi". A simple event but let us break down the psychology behind the act.

Firstly, my world was small. I was totally associated with the virtual world (in this case, watching the TV show). And I totally thought what I was shown was right. The fact that I ended up painting the sky and the mountain blue with only the pencil bordering the mountains to show the differentiation, points out to the fact that the mind is still unformed and unfurled by the world.

Secondly, the adult aspect of my mom being flabbergasted at my drawing also shows the conditioning that we are expected to have as we tend to grow old.

Third, going by the fact, mountains are supposed to be painted in a particular way but the way a child sees things are entirely different from how an adult perceives the world.

The conclusion from this aspect of life is that in this particular phase of life, we are all just learning. The inner child of the child has no conflicts to face and is just growing, following its own path.

THE SOCIAL BUILDUP

The later stages of childhood, paves the way for the future social interactions that the child will have in later stages of his life. This stage of life is crucial again. In this particular stage of life the child has been accustomed with the world. He is relatively stable and now his intelligence quotient starts developing further. This is because his relative intelligence increases as he sees more of the world, and starts differentiating between what is right and wrong in his own mind. Now whether the child will pursue the right value or the wrong value will again depend on what actions were taken on the child when he made decisions in his earlier phases of his life. If he was reprimanded often, the child will develop a regressive attitude or a depressed attitude. He will now either assume whatever decisions he are taking to be wrong or to be totally correct. There is no midway here. This aspect of life brings us to the more decisive part of life which is the intelligence quotient. The intelligence quotient is hard to define as it will vary constantly depending on the experience the person has. Yet to define it in a graph, it will be something like the below graph.

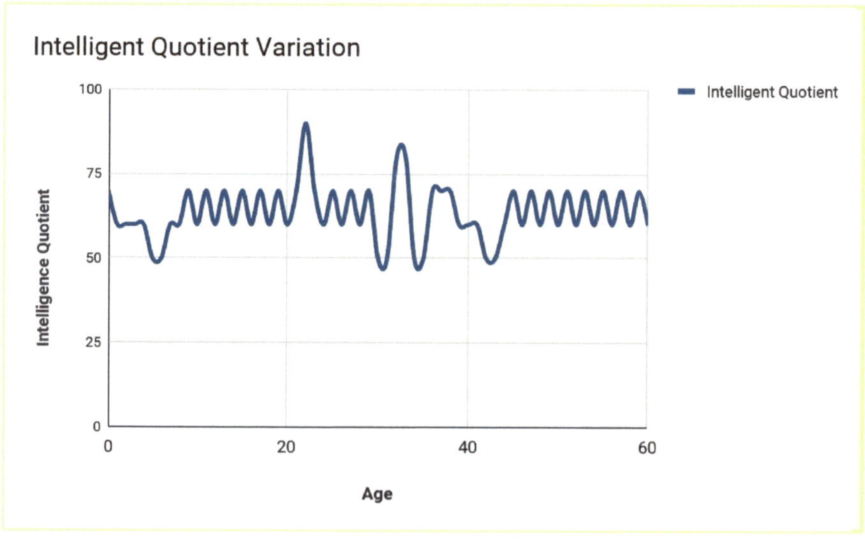

Again as with the previous graphs before, don't take the numbers into account. It is more of the pattern that I will concentrate on here. The intelligence quotient takes a dip in the initial years of childhood. This is because you are questioning your very own existence here and learning a lot of new things. Then your intelligence kind of starts fluctuating having cyclical tendencies. Now it spikes up as you turn into an adult. This is because at that age, you tend to perceive things in a different way. The atrocities of life strike you hard and you have decisions to make. But the good news is that you are now equipped to handle those adversities in life and also to find the beauty life has to offer in the midst of adversity. Point to be noted here, don't confuse the intelligence quotient I am mentioning over here with the measure of intelligence that is being carried on in the world. As I have mentioned before the metric I am using here doesn't go above 100 and the numbers are pretty arbitrary. Also the numbers illustrating the pattern are generic and are created by me to represent the general masses. If you consider yourself to be an outlier, then awesome.

So let's now merge the graphs and see how the different quotients I have mentioned varies in life.

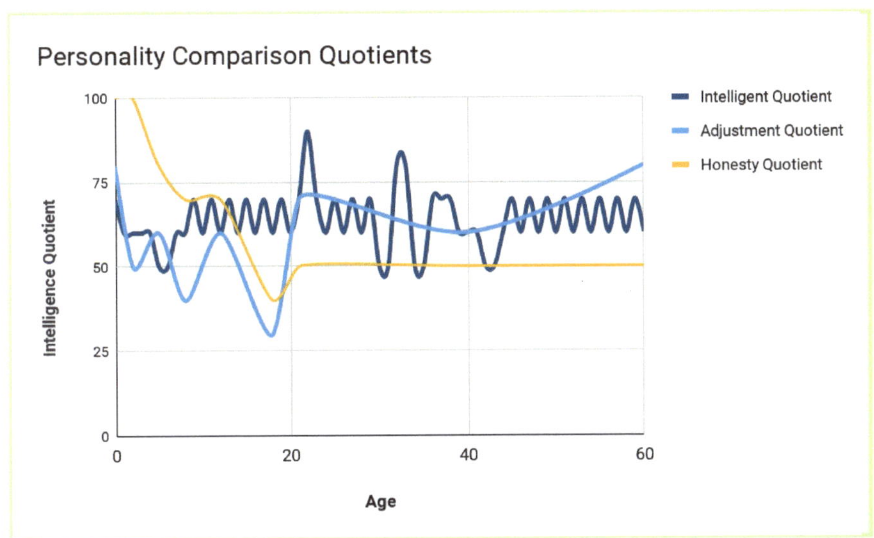

I guess you might have observed it already. The honesty quotient suffers the most as we progress in life. By suffering, I not only mean the value of it but also the logic that it remains relatively steady. On the other hand, the intelligent quotient varies all the time even in cyclic form factor. Let's concentrate on these two factors first and then we can go into the adjustment factor.

We can now say looking at these graphs, that intelligence of ours is cyclic and just like the seasons come one after the other, our intelligence varies consistently. If you want to test my theory out, do a simple task as simple as cutting a potato. If you have done it several times before, you will do it in the exact same way that you have been doing it in the past. But if you are doing it for the first time, you keep doing it several times till you actually saturate out and keep doing it the same way. You might wonder how this is related to the cyclical pattern I was just mentioning. But the fact of the matter is that the very choice you're making to do it right and get it fit for your action (i.e. fixing on how to cut the potato) is itself a cyclical action where your varied intelligence is put to the test. Feel free to disagree.

Onto the honesty quotient. The reason why this quotient saturates is our values get built with time and gets fixed. It is important to note that during early childhood, the nurturing that takes place plays a vital role in shaping up of the personality of honesty in a person. This quotient seldom varies. It is important to know something important in life. There are few basic instincts we have and are born with which will not change with time. The term congenital is as a result used. On the other hand, the above three personalities can be developed with time and is often the result of interactions that we have in our lives. We should choose to respond in our lives and not react to it. More on this, later.

Now let's delve deep into the social buildup that takes place. Society influences a lot of decisions that are being taken by the child. The mental formation of the child depends on the society. If the culture of the society the child is brought up in has a dearth of values, then the child tries to inculcate those values within himself. This is detrimental not only for the child but as well as for the people surrounding the child. It is important to look at things from a long range developmental perspective. The childhood years plays a major role in a psychological buildup of the child. But the interesting quotient that now comes up as a child slowly starts transitioning to the adult life is the anger quotient. And yes the anger quotient just pops up. The anger quotient was always there from the beginning of the birth but was literally living a dormant life till the child actually starts to go into the adult phase of his life. As it can be seen from the above graphs, it is pretty clear that there are drastic changes that occur during the transition to the teenage phase. And this kind of natural as the hormonal changes kind of take place at this kind of age. It is important to know the repercussions this has on the social buildup of the person. Suddenly the approval and guidance of the parents become annoying. Search for freedom and independence begins and as a result a tendency to revolt begins. As a result, the adjustment quotient goes for a big toss here. It is important for the people around to understand that this behaviour is normal and if unchecked can result in drastic consequences. This is the tender age in which people get the notion of becoming cool in front of their peers. The need for showing that they themselves are better kind of oozes out and this creates a lot of issues. Let's look into the issues that our newly entered teenage person faces.

As the child progresses from childhood into the stream of teenage years, he feels a mixed burden of emotions rushing through him. These emotions are basically a turmoil of the different personality traits that are existing within the child from birth. In the early teenage years, the child is now suddenly realizing the need for approval from the opposite gender. The modern world has kind of overemphasized this transition and has become over protective or over liberal of this situation and as a result the criminal actions taken by teenagers have risen a lot in the recent years. Going into the psychology behind it actually proves that often it is no fault of the teenagers themselves. They were dealt badly during their childhood and their personality has developed a twisted turn. Going back to the graphs, the other quotient values gets lowered during this period except the anger quotient. This suddenly takes a spike. The need for proving the identity kind of increases and as a result, any opposition to this is dealt badly and with anger. Let's see how the graph for the anger quotient will now look like.

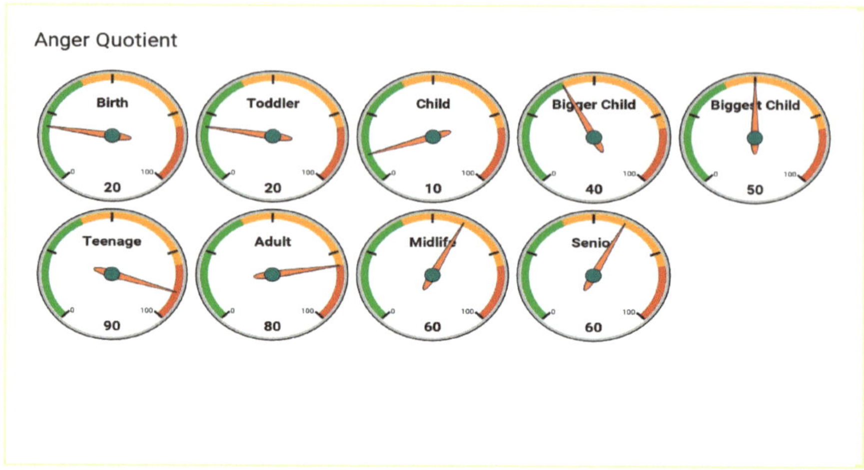

I had to put up this speedometer thing mainly for two reasons. First to highlight that compared to the other quotient, higher value for this quotient is actually bad and hence the red signal for it. And car speedometers are cool. (I wonder why I still like the analog ones even though we are all trying to go digital in this day and age).And also just like the honesty quotient, this quotient also kind of tapers and saturates. The point to be noted here is that during the teenage years, the anger quotient hits the red line and is at its max. The reason for this is very simple. The teenage mind has hit enough levels of understanding to develop its own identity yet it hasn't given a synopsis to what the brain has seen over the years. In simpler terms, it is confused as to what it wants to do. You might not have experienced any confusion during your teenage years, and if you haven't, then the sole reason is that you were raised very properly. Raised is a big term though, but I will still use the common nomenclature to make things simpler.

The need for creating a strong identity overpowers intelligence here. The ability to reason out of situation takes a toll. It is generally at this age, the uncontrolled mind look for other things to latch on to. But I am not citing that all teenagers are bad and they have an unformed mind. My objective here is to depict that though the person at this age might think they can achieve everything and anything and can do whatever they can and get away with it, they are wrong. So what needs to be done then?

The most important thing is for the parents to take care of the child now. The parents are often forced to think that their child has grown up enough to manage his own stuff. It is important to know that they are partially correct here. A balance between freedom and restrictions are needed. If left unchecked, life can go for a toss. Most of my friends started drinking and making out at this age. I am not saying that it is bad. The problem is control. When your inner mind wants something, you should try to get it. But too much of anything is bad. One glass of beer is fine but 20 jugs of beer is definitely not. The task of the parents mainly lies in making the child understand the difference between too much and too little. If at 16 years of age a teenage guy is ranting at whatever he sees, then it could be because his liberty was taken away. On the other hand if the same teenage boy is all too quiet, chances are he is putting up a masked version of himself out in the world. This is even deadlier as this can actually lead to psychological imbalance. Creating the fine balance is necessary to enjoy life. If you are overdoing something, it requires check. Teenagers feel more entitled. Their notions of life keep changing with every little thing they come across at this tender age. For the teenagers to grow up without nagging problems of substance abuse, of being addicts at whatever they are doing, it is important that they spend time in a relaxed manner. The access to a lot of information at the palm of the hand of the teenagers through mobiles , laptops and other gadgets have resulted into the teenagers feeling more entitled and have put them into a field of competition that they were not supposed to go into. Let's take an example of a modern day teenager.

This teenager has all the necessities of life met. He has food, he has shelter, he has a group of friends and he has people around him. The difference is he opens up a new account in Instagram, sees some of his peers holidaying in the Bahamas and starts sobbing and calling life is unfair. I believe there is a problem here. **Comparison is the evil** that is existing in this world at this moment. I believe every individual in this world has their own special abilities. Comparison kind of forces to channelize one's strength and weakness into being someone they are totally not. This is the fundamental problem I feel that is existing with the current society. Just because another person is holidaying in Bahamas, doesn't mean your life sucks. Your life is different just like everyone else's. It is important to have gratitude for whatever you have. Making the teenage adult understand this at this very age is important. Mind you I am not the guy who will tell you that you should leave all worldly desires, become a saint and live in the Himalayas. Sure that is possibly a way to live but I am just not that guy. From my perspective, it is important to find happiness in life and sustain it no matter what life throws you.

Now that we are partially aware of the problems that exists with life, let me tell something simple. Life doesn't exactly suck. We are only complaining because we are feeling entitled. The more we complain, the more entitled and narcissistic we are actually. We should calm down and make something for ourselves here. We should take a few minutes from our busy lives and just introspect. Some habits are formed over the years and will take a lot of time to go away. But the trick here is to recognize what habits of yours are detrimental not only for you, but for the people around you. It is important to know the second aspect. Often, we are so self-centered that we tend to ignore the people that are helpful to us and we are often not grateful. That kind of needs to change. I believe this a part of evolutionary process which is often neglected. Moving onto the adult life that has a lot of saturation involved with it.

ADULTHOOD

Adulthood is the phase of our lives for which we are living the longest duration. By this time, our identity is properly defined and we try to hold on it no matter what the cost. I will divide the basic constituent of life into three things.

1. **Need**
2. **Want**
3. **Greed**

Let's elucidate further on this. All the earlier years of life, you are generally taken care of. But now since you are considered a grown up, you are expected to manage your own things and become someone in life. This concept of becoming someone has been overhyped in the modern world in my opinion. It is perfectly fine to live life just as it is. I am not saying that you should just become no one in life and not pursue any goals and just keep sitting idle at home. No, that is not my point of view. But my perspective is that in the modern age, it is important to keep things at your own pace and work slowly towards something that you believe in without being fettered by what the world thinks about you. As we become adults, the importance of money becomes clearer to us. A person can be blissfully happy even if he has less money whereas a person can be extremely sad even if he has a lot of money. All of this boils down to the constituents of life I have just mentioned above.

Need refers to both materialistic as well as emotional aspects of your life which are totally necessary for survival. In other words they are indispensable. Let's take an example. If a person requires a mobile phone to connect with his relatives and friends just for talking and taking some photographs, he can buy a phone which is worth 100$ and get all his purpose served. This defines the need aspect of his life. Now if that same person requires a better quality phone which has some AI based capabilities enabled, he will look for a phone worth 400$. This is the want aspect. The next, is wanting the absolute best. This is the greed aspect. It is worth noting that a person's need and to an extent want can always be satisfied but a person's greed can never be satisfied. Now here again, I am not saying that you should live life as minimalistic way as possible, but what I am suggesting that you got to ask yourself three questions before you want to buy anything in life.

1. **Will I become sad if I don't own it?**
2. **Does it improve my quality of life?**
3. **Can I buy at least 3 of the same items?**

If you answer No, to any one of these questions, then in my honest opinion, you can still live your life fine without purchasing them. For example, you don't have a car. You really want to buy a car. Ask yourself the questions. As I have mentioned before, one should seek happiness. If you believe that buying a car will give you absolute happiness then go ahead and do it. But in that process you also need to ask whether you end up in huge loans in the process. The reason for the third question is that you should have enough to splurge on in order to think that you can splurge on.

So all these explanations and examples, where does this lead to in the adult life? The point is simple. It leads to the fact that in our adult life we need to see if what we are doing is absolutely necessary for survival or not. As we transition from the need to impress peers to become a bit more self-reliant, we fail to understand ourselves completely. At adult age, we are looking for our partner, we are still looking for reliance but yet we want to be independent. It is here that the conflict kind of starts.

Going into an example from my life, when I was in my early adulthood, things weren't going well for me. Materialistic things were there and I was fortunate enough to have them but I felt that I had failed somewhere in life (what this is, requires a lot of explanations which I am unwilling to do). As a result of this fear, I started feeling the need to rely on someone else. As I got into my undergraduate college, my life was literally into a mess as I kept thinking that I have failed in life and felt the very need to die. I used to be a decent student who was generally good in mathematics, and one fine day in college, I got 10 out of 30 in a math's exam. I was depressed. I was ashamed of myself. I just told this marks to only one friend of mine who was very close to me back then. (And still she is). Another friend of mine (who was pretty sure he got the highest marks), asked my friend how much I got. She replied, "Whatever Trambo has got he has got, it is none of your business." And I got to know this from her (And was also confirmed by this guy as well). As a result, I started overly relying on her. I felt that someone was helping me without myself asking for it. This created a dependency. In adult life it is important not to be too dependent on people. But is important to be dependent on people to an extent. And that again is perfectly fine. I have this philosophy with respect to life. Treat yourself like a movie star. A movie star has a lot of fans, a lot of critics but they go out there and perform the role that they are supposed to perform without thinking of the repercussions. It is like building a wall around yourself. This is important.

Also a very important skill in life is learning to say "No*". This is a skill which requires mastery. You might argue that you can easily say no to things which you don't want, but it is not that simple. Once you develop some sort of attachment to people, you always tend to think that telling no or not agreeing with them may be detrimental for the relationship that exists between the two of you. That is why learning to say "No*" as an asterisk associated with it. You should learn to say "No" without hurting the other person. A way to this is often setting low expectations from your end. This involves, self-criticizing. If you criticize yourself a lot, you will know what the faults in yourself are and will as a result give a proper image to the other people who are around you and are working with you. Learning to say "No" maybe a skill which can take a lifetime to master. One should be aware of the fact that saying "No" doesn't always mean that you are being rude and harsh. It means that you love yourself enough to protect yourself from adversities that you are expecting.

In adult life, a person is always looking for some sort of security. This is an innate search for the evolution of humankind to take place. Technology develops very fast these days and keeping up with it has become a necessity. But in my opinion, the modern age kind of forces you into competition. This is detrimental for health in my opinion. One should compete only when one is willing to compete. Sadly, in the modern society, people are all striving to be the best. People should strive away. But they should be striving to be the best version of themselves. Comparison with others itself kills the creativity of the mind and results into imitation mentality.

This brings me to another quotient. The 5th one, yes the ignorance quotient. Let's see how the graph of ignorance quotient is here.

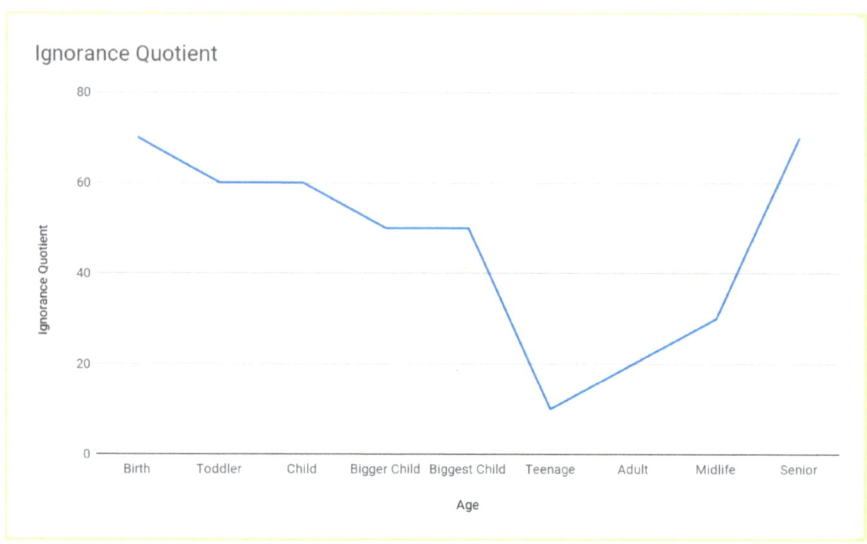

The ignorance chart is interesting. In my opinion we should have a balanced ignorance quotient. Too much ignorance quotient, implies that we are totally unaware of our surroundings. One may get hit by a truck on the road if he is so blissfully ignorant all the time. On the other hand a very low ignorance quotient implies one is fettered by anything and everything around him. That also possess an issue that the person will not have mental peace as he is constantly thinking about what others are thinking and is constantly developing a reaction based actions. As we become adults, we tend to think what others are thinking about us more than ever before. Because now another aspect comes into our life. This is known as ego. You may ask why ego is not treated as a fundamental personality. I believe ego is formed with experiences. You take two toddlers and give them something to play with. They will start playing and enjoying each other's company irrespective of caste, creed, religion and what not. If you tell the same toddlers to play with each other when they are teenagers, they may not be willing to do it. This is because by this time, their identity is partially formed and they are now totally dependent on defending it. This problem aggravates further when one gets older.

The graph kind of indicates that as we are becoming adults we tend to ignore very little and try to be aware as much as possible. But as we grow old, we get experienced enough to start ignoring things all over again. The striking similarity comes in the form of childhood and old age. They are strikingly similar.

Adulthood comes with a lot of irony in life. I will try to cite a few examples to illustrate them. Moving on to the next chapter.

THE IRONIES OF LIFE

"Damn, I want it now." We have often experienced this feeling in our lives. Let us understand that every moment of our lives we will be facing new challenges and new experiences both good and bad. The values that we should cultivate should make us aloof of the desire of instant gratification. We need to understand something's in life do take their own time. And we must have the skill to have the patience to bear it.

A common example is this so called phenomenon of love and linkages. You can like a person and that person can like another person and that person might end up liking you back. A complete cycle.

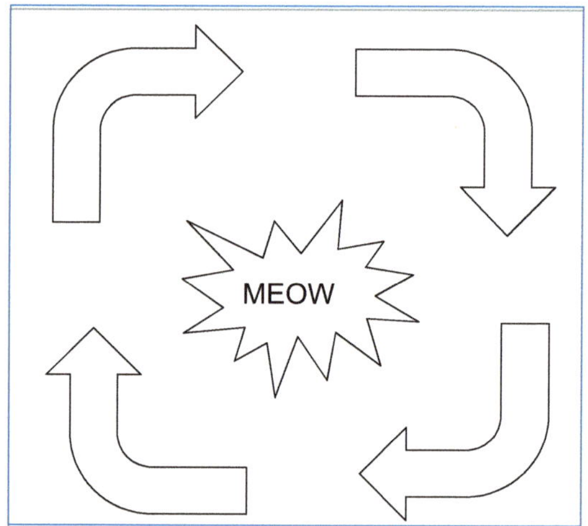

I would like to call this the meow cycle. Because I just want to call it. The dependency cycle in life is not only for such a thing but for many other things. It brings me to the deadlock concept I had read in my engineering days. Life will have a lot of dependencies involved and it is important to make yourself self-reliant. This is a difficult task to accomplish my friend. There will always be dependency but how less dependent you are on others determine how peaceful you will be.

Just like the little drops build up the ocean, the little things in life will help you to achieve self-reliance. Now comes the irony of life.

Just when you think everything is going well in life, you could be hit by a storm out of nowhere. It is similar to the calm before the storm scenario.

It is important to build up mental peace. To do that, it is important to become oblivious to the external factors in your life. No matter how good of a person you are, there are some things which will always be out of your control and you will have to live with the consequences it possess. For example, you gave your best in an exam, expected that you will get everything correct and get a 100 out of 100. But when your results came you saw you got 73 out of 100. You might wonder what happened when you suddenly realized that the last 6 pages of your paper got lost in transition. (A very unlikely situation you might wonder but it is likely even in the slightest margins.) The point I am trying to get here is that there are some things which are not under your control and you have to bear the results the situation gives you. The important thing here is not to lose your mind over it.

I will kind of revert back to the anger quotient a bit here. If a person has always a very high angry quotient at any point of his life, does it mean the person is bad? The answer is no. It is good to be angry at times. It is good to vent out anger at times. But it is also important to keep in check that the anger quotient doesn't damage the surroundings or the people around you. You suddenly become angry and start throwing and smashing things around you because of things not going your own way is a problem. Personally I have never done such things except two instances. When I look back at it now, I still feel embarrassed. I had ended up breaking a door after the girl I like just refused to talk to me and wanted her own space. That also indicates another thing, the excessive rise of the ego factor. The other instance was when I was playing a video game and my mom just pulled the charging cable of my laptop and I lost the match. I ended up throwing my laptop which resulted into it getting permanently damaged. When I look back at both of the instances, I find it very silly and stupid that I acted on reactionary forces without any self-control. In life it is important to respond to situations rather than react. Before you get angry at anything, it is important to ask yourself a few questions and just calm down.

1. **Can I be angry at this situation all my life?**

2. **Can this anger cause damage to anyone?**

3. **Can this anger be avoided?**

Most probably your answer to the above questions will be No, Yes and Yes respectively. The outcome is simple here, you can just relax down now. There is no point in getting angry. If you have an answer Yes, to the first question, that implies you have now the need to channelize this anger into something productive. By productive I mean something which you feel good doing. It could be painting, dancing and anything in this world which makes you happy without damaging others. I keep mentioning this over and over again. Enjoy life and do whatever you want without hurting others. That will give you solace.

You might wonder why I suddenly raised this perspective of anger when I am happily discussing about Ironies of Life. Welcome to Mismanagement Lion. It is when you get angry, the lion inside you starts to roar and you will realize it is at that point of time you will feel most results are not going your way. As you feel results are not going your way, the entitlement factor comes in and as a result you start looking for alternatives to latch on to. In other words, escape the reality.

The Mismanagement Lion will direct you towards things which have instant gratification attached towards it. The example of me breaking the door or throwing away the laptop is a classic case of the Mismanagement Lion acting as the predator. In our lives, we often fail to curtail the desires of the Mismanagement Lion. I have been playing video games for over two decades and it has made me realize the constant urge to be victorious is another gameplay by the Mismanagement Lion. You may wonder why it is so. The tendency to always be victorious is channeled more by the anger quotient. The need for identity comes across and failures are often handled badly. One of my close friends had suggested to me that I handled failures very badly. And damn, she was totally correct. Handling failures is another skill which requires to be built up. And the reason why this thing is titled under the ironies of life, is because when you are trying too hard to achieve something, chances are you will fail. You may argue that this is not true. The truth value of the statement is definitely debatable here but from what I have seen in life, I personally feel when we are trying to overdo things, we are hell bent on the result than that of the process. It is like we imagine the end result of viewing the world from the top of Mt. Everest.

At 8,848 meters the view will surely look awesome. But we seldom remember the process it will take to reach that height. You could even fall down while climbing, there could be landslides, snowstorms and maybe even yeti loitering (yes exaggeration but well.....). The point is, it is good to know about what the summit holds for you but it is also equally important to know what it takes to reach the summit. The capabilities of persons vary from men to men and women to women and that must be taken into account before taking judgments on how to proceed with the process for reaching a goal.

When you are down and out, it is time for that one last try. Often we don't end up realizing our true potential because we fear trying out. It is important to fail and try. And I guess you have heard this over a thousand times but I still wanted to highlight it anyway. What I would like to add up here that if you embark on a new journey, try and read about the failure stories attached with it. (Obviously if you are planning to start a startup company with a completely new technology, you won't get such stories). The reason why I cite this is that though failure gives you an experience from which you can improve upon, why fail at all when you can avoid it? Going back to climbing Mt. Everest, the trekkers take enough oxygen with them because it is expected that oxygen levels will fall down. How is this known? From past experiences and science. So the point I am trying to get here is, **"You can be successful without failing if you give your hundred percent in planning"**.

As Mismanagement Lion will try to channelize your behaviour in a multitude of ways, you will feel the rise of another aspect of your life. Escapism. The entitled part of ourselves make us want to escape whenever there is a problem. The ability to face problems is a hidden quality that every person has. To tame the Mismanagement Lion is essential for realizing our true potential.

WHAT SHOULD WE DO

Before answering the question, what we should do, we should ask ourselves, do we really have a problem in our life? We seldom have gratitude towards the things we already have and always end up chasing things losing our peace of mind, making our anger quotient go up and become narcissistic and egoistic. We may often lose peace of mind for no apparent reason.

We should distance ourselves enough from things which constantly hurts us. We should have a veil around us that protects us from the damage of the inner child within us. But there should be differentiation with respect to the characteristic of ego over here. An issue that we face is that we are often bounded by the expectations people have around us. We try to live up to the expectation that people have of us and often forget that we have some expectations of ourselves as well.

I remember a friend of mine told that her family was always expecting too much out of her. She told her story of how she coped up with it and ultimately didn't give a damn to it. Interestingly, she grew better with time. Today she is a very successful person doing a lot of stuff, managing a lot of things. (I am not going into specific details here). The point is as she set aside the expectations of others, she set a standard for herself. To me, she is a great example of a fighter and has been an awesome ideal person from whom a lot can be learnt from.

Like her, most of us have several expectations being set on us. We try to live up to them and in return forget our true selves. I will illustrate this with a world map. You may wonder why. More on this, soon enough. (Yes, wanted to be different here).

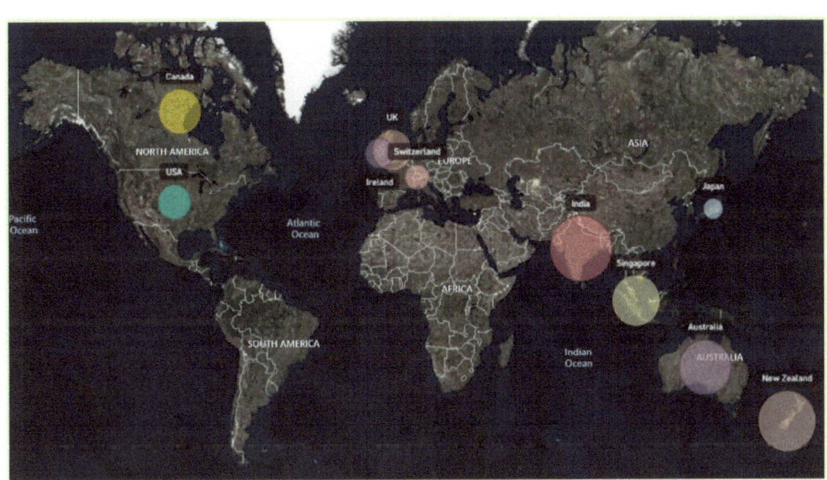

Let's say that we are born in one of the countries. For example, in my case it is India. Let us all have our basic expectations from us being set as the country we are born in. That will always have the highest value. This is represented as the size of the bubble in the world map. Now what do I mean by basic here?

When we are born, our parents immediately start having several expectations from us. This expectations often can act as a channelizing force which determines how we proceed. What I plot away in the map is that apart from this basic expectations, all other expectations are set by different people and they have different weights. Let's map some of our expectations with the different countries.

Base expectations–   India

Friend's expectations–   New Zealand

Relative's expectations–   Australia

Workplace expectations–   Singapore

Unknown expectations–   Canada

Senior's expectations–   UK

Own expectations–   The other countries

     If you notice, the own expectations have the smallest size of the bubbles across the various countries. The point that I am trying to highlight here can be divided into two.

1. We set aside our own expectations and keep working for others. I am not telling you to be selfish here and just put your expectations above anyone else. But it is important to have your expectations set right. To know what one is expecting of themselves is an arduous task too. And the funny part is our expectations of ourselves can change with time. If a challenge that we thought we would be able to handle was too much for us, then we can often lead ourselves into believing that we should set our expectations lower. This, I believe is incorrect. **Never ever think you are not capable enough to achieve your own expectations.** One sets their own expectations because they believe they can achieve it.

2. The other countries highlighted here are pretty far away in the distance. What I am trying to highlight here is that our wants are varied across space. (Denoted by the spread across different countries).

     The point is that we should try to highlight our requirements as well. It is very important that we know what we want in life. You might have heard of several people telling you to set a goal in life. Pursue it and so on and so forth. I personally have a different opinion. I believe once you start enjoying what you are doing, the goal kind of gets set automatically. In the context of what we should do, we should always remember that what we should do, should not harm others in the short run or in the long run.

     I would like to reiterate something that I mentioned before but now I will like to give it a title. Let's call this the Veil of Shadow. Yes, kind of a weird name but what I'm trying to say here is that we should have our defenses ready while developing our goals. The Veil of Shadow should help us understand that beyond our colloquial life, we are someone who we wish to become. It is therefore essential that we live true to ourselves. The camouflaging that occurs on us and binds us to do things that we don't want to do, becomes our reality which is totally unacceptable in my opinion. I'll mention a short poem here that I had written more than a decade back.

"You were there when everyone was away,

You were there when everybody refused to stay,

You were there when I was cold,

You were there when I was bold.

I was missing the moment of my life,

As I always wanted to strive,

To the goals and goals ahead,

Didn't matter whether I was beheaded.

My success today is virtually yours,

As you always been by my side,

Never ever try to tell a lie to you,

Cause you are my only human mind. "

The highlight of this poem is that being true to yourself is essential. Also in my opinion, rarely lie. The reason I am saying rarely instead of never is simple. Ideal situations rarely exists in life.

Avoid lying as much as possible. The reason I am telling this is that we are wired to often think that we can escape by telling the lies. Let me tell you this, telling lies will deplete your ROM. Yes, I had to use a computer science reference. The more you lie, you have to retain all the information that you have lied. Unnecessary wastage of your memory space in my opinion. I can tell you one thing, telling lies is another way of escapism. More on this, later.

In life as we grow older, we get more experiences and we feel a little bit more comfortable with our identity. Back in the days, a friend of mine used to like a girl. He was always thinking about her and would often trouble all his close friends citing only her examples in the very little things of life. Now she didn't have any feelings for him and to him that was actually creating a hole in him and in simpler words hurting his ego. It is okay if the girl or boy you like, doesn't like you back. It is okay to let them go and move on. It is okay to cry a little and feel that the world is crashing down. It is perfectly okay. The reason why I am citing this is during those days he felt that he had no purpose in his existence and his sole purpose of living was only her, his happiness depended on her and there were such dependencies. But as life progressed, he realized that things which were so important to him at some point of time, become very insignificant as time progressed. Sure enough, you will have a lot of painful memories associated but in my opinion concentrate on the brighter side of things.

Back in my school days, I used to live in a hostel and the warden would wake all of us up early in the morning at 5:30 am by frantic banging of the room doors. 5:30 am might seem a good time to wake up for some but for me it was devastating at that point of time because

1. I slept after 2 am and

2. I was lazy and the perfect procrastinating teenager

I used to be so irritated by the banging of the door that I felt like running away but I didn't have options. The memories are still there, but now when I look back, I can easily call them the funny days. Back then, they were torture. So the point I am trying to highlight here is that with the passage of time our life heals, fits in well. What seems so important today, you may be blissfully ignorant about it a few years down the line. Few days back I was so surprised when I realized that a song that I used to hear on loop a decade ago, were no longer on my playlist. I suddenly came across it while browsing through my files on my computer and it amazed me that even something I loved and had no bad memories of, had simply disappeared into the thin air. This is the paradox of life in my opinion. Memories, whether good or bad, can be easily forgotten if a better present comes in its place.

So the big question about "What should we do?" We should not escape. Yes, I am being blatant here. We all have the tendency to escape from reality albeit each of us having a different proportion attached to it. We need to embrace changes. There are some things in life you will definitely have no control over. I will go back to the example of the friend of mine about the girl he liked. He was giving his all, trying to help her in all ways possible, trying to highlight to her every single time how she was very important to him and what not. But she was always clear that she didn't like him the way he liked her. He still pursued on like a fool. In other words for him, the escapism was her. And that is a terrible mistake one can do. Learning from my experience, I can tell that it is good to escape the mundane functions of life but escape into something which will have no return associated with it. In his case, he was expecting the girl to like him back and you know how things follow. The fact of the matter is that by concentrating on a person to be your escapism, the virtual reality that he was creating for himself was itself a dependent variable. Never make escapism a dependent variable.

The moment you create an escaping reality which has dependencies other than yourself, you are basically creating the need for another escapism. So this will actually cause a chain reaction to something like the one illustrated in the following diagram.

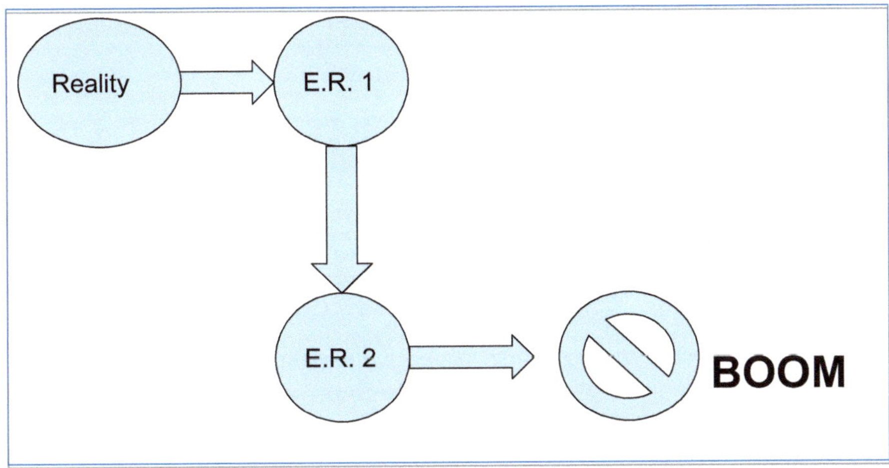

As you try to escape from reality, you go into the escaping reality one, trying to escape from the new escaping reality, you go into escaping reality part 2 and before you know it you are in a vicious chain from which you are not able to get away and "Boom" explosion and you are suddenly into depression. The problem here is most of us are too afraid to face our problems. Facing our problems takes courage. If we are just avoiding the problems, it doesn't mean that we will reach the solution. We need to solve the problem by digging down deeper into the root cause. You might argue that some problems will not have a solution. True, there are things which will leave some permanent spots in your life which cannot be avoided. But evading from them will not solve the problem. We should embrace our problems and feel good that we have those problems. Embracing the problem will give you the courage to face it. It will reduce the entitlement attitude that exists within ourselves. It is okay to be wrong at times, it is okay to be vulnerable, it is okay to look into the stars and it is perfectly okay to gobble a 12 inch pizza all by yourself.

Another thing we often tend to overlook is how we tend to become possessive with the people we love and start taking them for granted. Being possessive is good but being over possessive is detrimental for the people around you. Back in my early days, I used to call my close friends and if they didn't pick up, I would get agitated and start telling them that they don't have time for me. The perfect childish attitude in my opinion. As I look back at those days now, there is no proper reason for getting agitated. It is important to give people their own little space and respect them enough. Along with this though, I feel we also need to do it for ourselves. We need to respect our own time. We take ourselves for granted. We might crib around at times thinking things are going wrong and we are not having control over it, but that will never solve the problem. It is good to escape at times but we shouldn't totally run away from reality. So I would modify the diagram I showed above.

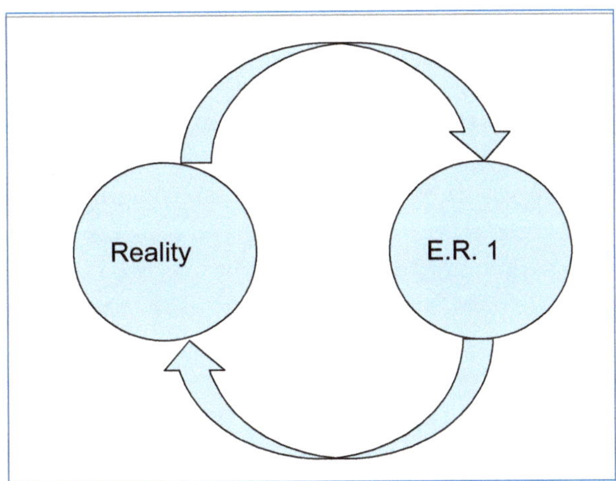

The most important thing I feel is that we should respond in life and not react. Think of your life as a highly aerated drink. You are now shaken（not stirred）. The moment the container is opened you fizz out, the spilling is everywhere and you gush out losing your very own essence. Instead, take the example of water. No matter how much you shake it, it will not gush out. We all know water is indispensable. The fact of the matter is that we can choose whether we want to become water or be fettered by everything that happens in our lives.

HOLDING ON TO THE INNER CHILD

As we grow up we are subjected to so much experiences that we seldom forget that these are the experiences that will shape our lives for the most part. The little things play a crucial role in shaping us into the person we are and they have some good reasons associated with it. So what do I mean by holding on to the inner child here? It is simple. It is that part of you to which no one should ever have access to change. For example, you are an inquisitive person who likes to question everything and everything. Just because others are saying that whatever questions you are asking are absolutely ridiculous, don't stop asking the questions. But rather than asking it in open forum, try to figure it out yourself first. In today's era, there are a lot of resources to figure out things. Holding on to the inner child basically refers to the part of you which defines you. Imagine every materialistic thing is taken away from you. The question now becomes who are you? We in this modern world are so focused on the materialistic aspect of things that we forget to attain inner solace. This can be a rather intriguing task. If you are holding on to the inner child, you will be unfettered by the world. Negative things will not impact you. Depression will not target you. This can be illustrated in a very simple way.

The sun inside is the real you. And the outer boundaries are the inhibitions you have from becoming you. The outer boundaries influence you to such an extent that you reduce your radiation and become a limited version of yourself. It is important to not let this inner child die down because of the outer boundaries. This can only be achieved if we are totally reliant on our virtues. Don't let other people take away "You" from you.

The reason why I cite this here, is something that I have mentioned before. We are often living a life we don't want to live. We want change. But let me tell you this and cause a heartbreak. Every change that you seek now will again be seeking another change after a while. You might have heard it a hundred times that "Change is the only constant". The problem with a change we seek is that the change is still in a masked form. What I imply here can be elucidated with an example. For example, you are a very successful person. (Let's take the normal definition of success here, materialistic things, and high positions and so on.) You will still have some goals ahead of you and try to achieve them. The question I would rather ask here, are these your goals or are they superimposed on you? The imposition can be from friends, family, peers and God knows who else. The point I am trying to get here is, if the changes and goals that you are searching after are not from the inner child within you, then you can never be satisfied with the changes that you have been doing and the challenges you have been winning. Even if you are at the peak of Mount Everest, you will still think you are standing on Mariana Trench.

In every aspect of life, don't set the goals. They will come automatically with the inner child within you. If you are having dearth of money, the inner child will form that goal for you. We have the special ability of adapting to the environment and surviving. Adapting to changes is a special ability that has helped the human race to survive for so long. Now the irony here is that though the inner child within you has set the goal for you, you will be heavily influenced by everyone around you. You will start raising the goal to a point where it becomes unrealistic. You may say that I am being a pessimistic person here but truth be told, our needs often get changed into wants and our wants often get changed into greed. (The point I was mentioning before). We as an individual will never have this problem but it is the societal pressure that causes these changes in us. Holding on to the inner child is the utmost requirement that we should have in our life. It is the key to our happiness and endurance to face circumstances we face in our lives.

I'll keep this chapter short because it is about time to tell about "More on this, later".

MORE ON THIS, LATER

The first time I talked about the "More on this, later" is in the context of infants feeling that they are always right. There is a paradox here. Infants have very little knowledge of the world. Whatever they see initially feels new, questionable and exciting. As a result they are often into the thinking that the world they see are limited and whatever they are now knowing is an absolute information. This leads them to believe that they are absolutely certain over everything that they know. This leads to the development of the belief system also. Gradually with time, this fundamental belief system gets questioned and the infant starts to adapt.

The next time I mention it, it is basically to highlight a simple thing. One's identity building up is crucial because it paves the way for protecting the inner child. It is also harmful because the protection wall is kind of taken out of proportions and becomes the "Ego". This becomes so catastrophic over a period of time, that people are willing to go to any extent to defend their own "Ego". I am a very egoistic person, and over time I realized that it is one of the main reasons I have problems in my life. It is a very challenging task, and I believe it is a lifelong journey for people to grow out of this self-made identity trying to protect the inner child. Truth to be told, the inner child needs to come out of the boundaries and not form a cocoon to protect itself.

As we grow older, we try to defend our "Ego". And it becomes such a disease over time that we tend to go to any extent to defend this fragile version of ourselves. This is the reason why dishonesty and lying comes into the picture. We try to masquerade ourselves from showing the vulnerable side. We fear judgment, we fear outcomes and we fear the truth. What we should rather think is let's not fear the truth rather fear the consequences of the lies. That will help us grow better.

With time, we become the herd. The curious case of the new born child disappears and a person who is bound by pointless boundaries are born. It is good to have boundaries. But those boundaries should be made by ourselves. Hurting someone (physically or mentally) is a choice you are trying to make. Always ponder on one thing.

Can you live happily without committing the action you are about to commit?

If you can, don't do. This will help you to realize that life is simple and indeed societal pressures can't take away one thing from you. "**You**".

As we become more and more accustomed to life, we start to react vehemently (albeit in a negative way) to defend our beliefs. We often forget that we should actually develop ourselves in such a way that we can actually respond. Responding involves the voluntary part of the response to an action. For example, if someone is trying to bully you, you can start feeling bad, go into depression and what not. But you can in turn make fun of yourself and agree with the people who are bullying you. What actually happens then? Bullies try to attain peace through defeat of others while they are very much aware of the fault they have. When you start laughing about yourself, the purpose that the bullies are trying to achieve get defeated. It is important sometimes to take a step back so that you can punch the obnoxious aspects of life with a thundering punch.

Telling lies builds up a world which doesn't exist. It is often done to form a superior image of one's own self. As I have mentioned before, it is perfectly fine to do a lot of stuff which has no impact on the world but completely is in line with your inner child. The inner child should seek solace in the truth and be happy in their own little spheres rather than building up an alternate reality which doesn't exist through lies.

So I have reached the end of all the sense and non-sense I had to offer. This book tries to put a perspective on life. There will be many things which you might feel that you already know. Agree to that, and I am sorry if reading this was a wastage of your time. My objective was to highlight things in a way which I feel is essential for smooth functioning. As always many things can be added on and this is no way a holistic coverage of what should be done and what should not be done.

To end, I would like to say something simple.

"Smile often, let the inner child in you be free of conflicts and wish you a very happy and peaceful life."

THE END